Autumn Leaf Half Gloves

or

How to Knit Fingerless Mitts

by

Janis Frank

Table of Contents

The inspiration of this pattern came from my previous Spider Fingerless Gloves pattern. I really like incorporating the design into the final wearable piece. I've always liked the leaf pattern and this seemed to be a great way to use it.

There isn't a full-on how to for this pattern, by I have included scannable QR codes to helpful videos to show you how to do certain parts of the pattern. These will certainly help with any of the tricker parts like knitting the wrong side of the YO K1 YO and drawing the edges of the leaves together to a point. To use the QR codes, take a photo with your smart phone or tablet. A link will pop up. Click the link and it will open and automatically play the YouTube video.

Gauge

This is important to follow for correct sizing. This is when using the US size 6 (4 mm) knitting needles in stockinette.

2" (5 cm) - 10 sts

2" (5 cm) - 15 rows

Things You Need

Knitting needles:

> Small - Size 3 US (3.25 mm) knitting needles
>
> Medium - Size 6 US (4 mm) knitting needles
>
> Large - Size 8 US (5 mm) knitting needles

Worsted weight yarn – any standard size ball will do

Cable Needle - There are a number a styles but I prefer the hook version

Stitch holder – It looks like a big safety pin

Tapestry needle

Sizing

Like my other fingerless mitt patterns, I've made this as one pattern and adjusted the needle size to change the sizes. This makes it a heck of a lot easier to design and keeps the proportion of the leaves the same on all sizes. Frankly, the overall look is better.

If you are making the small or large size glove, check the gauge for the size 6 US (4 mm). Adjust to the size of the needles to obtain the correct gauge. If you are making the large size, increase your needle size by a size US (mm). For example, you need to use a size 7 US (4.5 mm) to get the correct gauge, use size 9 US (5.5 mm) knitting needles for the large. If you are making a small, use size 5 US (3.75 mm).

To know what size you should make, you can use the info graphic below on how to measure your hand, or the hand of whomever you are making them for.

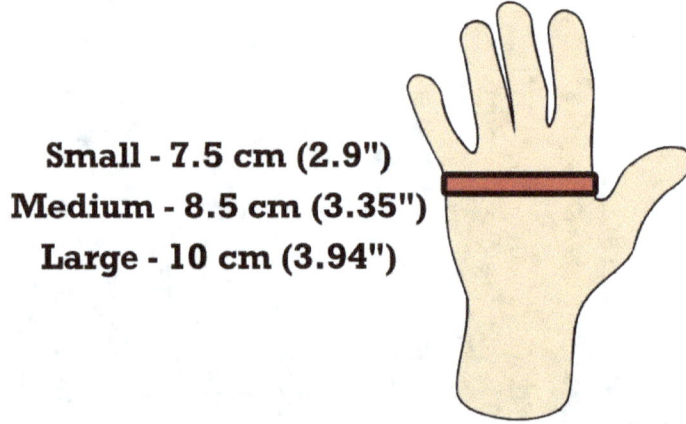

Small - 7.5 cm (2.9")
Medium - 8.5 cm (3.35")
Large - 10 cm (3.94")

Left Hand

Cast on 34

Row 1: (P1 K2) Repeat to last st. P1

Row 2: (K1 P2) Repeat to last st. K1

♥ **Row 3:** (P1 TB) Repeat to last st. P1

Row 4: As row 2 ♥ Repeat from ♥ to ♥ 3 times more. (Counts as rows 5-10).

Row 11: P1 P2tog P21 K3 P7 (33 sts)

Row 12: K7 P3 K23

Row 13: P23 K2 C1F P6

Row 14: K6 P1 K1 P2 K23

Row 15: P23 K2 P1 C1F P5

Row 16: K5 P1 K2 P2 K23

Row 17: P22 C1B K1 P2 YO K1 YO P5 (35 sts)

*Scan this code for help
make the YO K YO*

Row 18: K5 P3 K2 P1 K1 P1 K22 (35 sts)

*Scan this QR code for help with P3.
(The back side of the YO K YO.)*

Row 19: P21 C1B P1 K1 P2 (K1 YO) twice K1 P5 (37 sts)

Row 20: K5 P5 K2 P1 K2 P1 K21 (37 sts)

Row 21: P21 K1 P2 K1 P2 K2 YO K1 YO K2 P5 (39 sts)

Row 22: K5 P7 K2 P1 K2 P1 K21 (39 sts)

Row 23: P21 K1 P2 K1 P2 K2tog (When making this stitch, pick up a stitch as if to knit. Twist the stitch and place it back on your non-working needle. Knit the 2 stitches together from right to left.) K3 K2tog (knit the stitches together from left to right.) P5 (37 sts)

Scan this QR code for help with K2tog.

Row 24: K5 P5 K2 P1 K2 P1 K21 (37 sts)

Row 25: P21 K1 P2 K1 P2 K2tog (like you did before: pick up, twist, knit right to left) K1 K2tog (knit left to right) P5 (35 sts)

Row 26: K5 P3 K2 P1 K2 P1 K21 (35 sts)

Row 27: P14 PM1 P1 PM1 P6 YO K1 YO P2 K1 P2 Sl St (as if to knit) K2tog (knit left to right) PSSO P5 (37 sts)

Row 28: K8 P1 K2 P3 K23 (37 sts)

Row 29: P23 (K1 YO) twice. K1 P2 K1 P8 (39 sts)

Row 30: K8 P1 K2 P5 K6 M1 K3 M1 K14 (41 sts)

Row 31: P25 K2 YO K1 YO K2 P2 K1 P8 (43 sts)

Row 32: K8 P1 K2 P7 K25 (43 sts)

Row 33: P14 PM1 P5 PM1 P6 K2tog (pick up, twist, knit right to left) K3 K2tog (knit left to right) P2 C1F P7 (43 sts)

Row 34: K7 P1 K3 P5 K27 (43 sts)

Row 35: P27 K2tog (pick up, twist, knit right to left) K1 K2tog (knit left to right) P3 K1 P7 (41 sts)

Row 36: K7 P1 K3 P3 K6 M1 K7 M1 K14 (43 sts)

Row 37: P29 Sl St (as if to knit) K2tog (knit left to right) PSSO P3 YO K1 YO P7 (43 sts)

Row 38: K7 P3 K33 (43 sts)

Row 39: P14 PM1 P9 PM1 P10 (K1 YO) twice K1 P7 (47 sts)

Row 40: K7 P5 K35 (47 sts)

Row 41: P35 K2 YO K1 YO K2 P7 (49 sts)

Row 42: K7 P7 K10 M1 K11 M1 K14 (51 sts)

Row 43: P37 K2tog (pick up, twist, knit right to left) K3 K2tog (knit left to right) P7 (49 sts)

Row 44: K7 P5 K37 (49 sts)

Row 45: P14 Pass the next 13 sts of the thumb gusset onto a stitch holder. P10 K2tog (pick up, twist, knit right to left) K1 K2tog (knit left to right) P7 (34 sts)

Row 46: K7 P3 K24 (34 sts)

Row 47: P24 Sl St (as if to knit) K2tog (knit left to right) PSSO P7 (32 sts)

Row 48: K across

Row 49: P across

Row 50: K across

Row 51: P2tog (K2 P1) to the end of the row

☺ **Row 52:** (K1 P2) Repeat to the last st. K1

Row 53: (P1 TB) Repeat to the last st. P1 ☺ Repeat from ☺ to ☺ once.

Cast off loosely on the **WRONG** side.

Thumb

Pick up the 13 stitches on the stitch holder with the WRONG side facing you. (See hints and tips for more info).

Row 1: Knit across

Row 2: Purl across

Row 3: Knit across

Cast off on the **RIGHT** side.

Sew seam along the side of the glove and the inside of the thumb. Work in ends.

*Read more FREE knitting patterns
on my website.*

Right Hand

Cast on 34

Row 1: (P1 K2) Repeat to last st. P1

Row 2: (K1 P2) Repeat to last st. K1

♥ **Row 3:** (P1 TB) Repeat to last st. P1

Row 4: As row 2 ♥ Repeat form ♥ to ♥ 3 times more. (Counts as rows 5-10).

Row 11: P7 K3 P21 P2tog P1 (33 sts)

Row 12: K23 P3 K7

Row 13: P6 C1B K2 P23

Row 14: K23 P2 K1 P1 K6

Row 15: P5 C1B P1 K2 P23

Row 16: K23 P2 K2 P1 K5

Row 17: P5 YO K1 YO P2 K1 C1F P22 (35 sts)

*Scan this code for help
make the YO K YO*

Row 18: K22 P1 K1 P1 K2 P3 K5 (35 sts)

*Scan this QR code for help with P3.
(The back side of the YO K YO.)*

Row 19: P5 (K1 YO) twice K1 P2 K1 P1 C1F P21 (37 sts)

Row 20: K21 P1 K2 P1 K2 P5 K5 (37 sts)

Row 21: P5 K2 YO K1 YO K2 P2 K1 P2 K1 P21 (39 sts)

Row 22: K21 P1 K2 P1 K2 P7 K5 (39 sts)

Row 23: P5 K2tog (When making this stitch, pick up a stitch as if to knit. Twist the stitch and place it back on your non-working needle. Knit the 2 stitches together from right to left). K3 K2tog (knit the stitches together from left to right.) P2 K1 P2 K1 P21 (37 sts)

Scan this QR code for help with K2tog.

Row 24: K21 P1 K2 P1 K2 P5 K5 (37 sts)

Row 25: P5 K2tog (pick up, twist, knit right to left) K1 K2tog (knit left to right) P2 K1 P2 K1 P21 (35 sts)

Row 26: K21 P1 K2 P1 K2 P3 K5 (35 sts)

Row 27: P5 Sl St (as if to knit) K2tog (knit left to right) PSSO P2 K1 P2 YO K1 YO P6 PM1 P1 PM1 P14 (37 sts)

Row 28: K23 P3 K2 P1 K8 (37 sts)

Row 29: P8 K1 P2 (K1 YO) twice. K1 P23 (39 sts)

Row 30: K14 M1 K3 M1 K6 P5 K2 P1 K8 (41 sts)

Row 31: P8 K1 P2 K2 YO K1 YO K2 P25 (43 sts)

Row 32: K25 P7 K2 P1 K8 (43 sts)

Row 33: P7 C1B P2 K2tog (pick up, twist, knit right to left) K3 K2tog (knit left to right) P6 PM1 P5 PM1 P14 (43 sts)

Row 34: K27 P5 K3 P1 K7 (43 sts)

Row 35: P7 K1 P3 K2tog (pick up, twist, knit right to left) K1 K2tog (knit left to right) P27 (41 sts)

Row 36: K14 M1 K7 M1 K6 P3 K3 P1 K7 (43 sts)

Row 37: P7 YO K1 YO P3 Sl St (as if to knit) K2tog (knit left to right) PSSO P29 (43 sts)

Row 38: K33 P3 K7 (43 sts)

Row 39: P7 (K1 YO) twice K1 P10 PM1 P9 PM1 P14 (47 sts)

Row 40: K35 P5 K7 (47 sts)

Row 41: P7 K2 YO K1 YO K2 P35 (49 sts)

Row 42: K14 M1 K11 M1 K10 P7 K7 (51 sts)

Row 43: P7 K2tog (pick up, twist, knit right to left) K3 K2tog (knit left to right) P37 (49 sts)

Row 44: K37 P5 K7 (49 sts)

Row 45: P7 K2tog (pick up, twist, knit right to left) K1 K2tog (knit left to right) P10 Pass the next 13 sts of the thumb gusset onto a stitch holder. P14 (34 sts)

Row 46: K24 P3 K7 (34 sts)

Row 47: P7 Sl St (as if to knit) K2tog (knit left to right) PSSO P24 (32 sts)

Row 48: K across

Row 49: P across

Row 50: K across

Row 51: P2tog (K2 P1) to the end of the row

☺ **Row 52:** (K1 P2) Repeat to the last st. K1

Row 53: (P1 TB) Repeat to the last st. P1 ☺ Repeat from ☺ to ☺ once.

Cast off loosely on the **WRONG** side.

Thumb

Pick up the 13 stitches on the stitch holder with the WRONG side facing you. (See hints and tips for more info).

Row 1: Knit across

Row 2: Purl across

Row 3: Knit across

Cast off on the **RIGHT** side.

Sew seam along the side of the glove and the inside of the thumb. Work in ends.

Abbreviations

K – knit

P – purl

YO – yarn over

TB – Pick up the stitch with your stitch holder. Hold the stitch at the back of your work. Knit the next stitch. Knit the next stitch. Knit the stitch from the stitch holder.

Watch how to do the twist back

C1B – Cable 1 back. Pick up next stitch on a cable needle. Pull this stitch to the **BACK** of your work. **Knit** the next stitch. **Purl** the stitch on the cable needle.

Watch how to do C1B

C1F – Cable 1 forward. Pick up the next stitch on a cable needle. Pull this stitch to the **FRONT** of your work. **Purl** the next stitch. **Knit** the stitch on the cable needle.

Watch how to do C1F

M1 – Make one (knit wise). Increase one stitch between the stitches. Pick up the yarn between the stitches. Twist slightly. Place it on your non-working needle. Knit the stitch. Watch this video to see how.

PM1 - Make one (purl wise). Increase one stitch between the purl stitches. Pick up the yarn between the stitches. Place it on your non-working needle. Purl the stitch as you regularly would. Watch this video to see how.

K2tog – How you do this depends where you are in the pattern. If you are making the right side of the leaf, knit right to left. If you are making the left side of the leaf, knit left to right. If you do it this way you eliminate the twisting of the stitch and the edge of the leaf flows evenly.

The k2tog are given for **RIGHT** handed knitters. If you are knitting left to right as a **LEFT** handed knitter, reverse the order that you knit the stitches together. K2tog from left to right then pick up, twist, knit from right to left.

Sl St – slip the stitch

PSSO – pass the slipped stitch over.

Hints and Tips

Make your seams as narrow as possible when sewing them. The bulkier the seam the more noticeable and possibly uncomfortable for the wearer.

Everything between and including the PM1 and M1 stitches form the thumb gusset.

When you are making the thumb, you MUST pick up the stitches from the wrong side. Pass the stitches from the stitch holder to the knitting needle then onto the other knitting needle so the wrong side facing you. If you don't do the second pass, you'll get a weird line.

Leave the cast off end of the finger cuff and the thumb longer so you can use it to sew up the seam along the side of the gloves and seam of the thumb, respectively.

The striped ombre versions of the gloves are done with Loops & Threads "Facets" yarn you can find at Michaels (as of the printing of this pattern). It's thin for a worsted weight yarn and I needed to use a 4.5 mm set of dpn's to get the sizing correct. Make sure to check your gauge and adjust accordingly!

Please be aware that these gloves look like the leaves are off center when they're not being worn. I actually redesigned them so the motif would be 2 stitches over because when they were on, they looked too close to the thumb. Sometimes designs are weird and the center of the design visually isn't the middle of the design mathematically or functionally. Ahhh! The joys of art...

Like all of my patterns you have my permission to sell and/or give away the physical items that you make using this pattern. You are NOT permitted to reprint or duplicate this pattern in any form unless you have obtained my written permission to do so.

If you have any questions, please feel free to leave a comment or send me your questions at kweenbee_crafts@hotmail.ca.

Help Support My Work!

Follow me on TikTok, Instagram, Twitter, Facebook, Pinterest and YouTube. Every follow, subscribe, thumbs up, like, heart and share help increase my popularity on the web and get more viewers to my work. It costs you nothing but helps me sooooo much!

If you would like to help a little more, you can always become a Website Member to download print over 36 patterns. Or you can support me by becoming a Patron on Patreon or you can make a single time donation at Buy Me a Coffee.

You can use any of these QR codes to find out more.

Website Member   Patreon   Buy Me a Coffee

More FREE knitting patterns on my website

This is the latest list of patterns I have on my website. It is an ever growing list so you might want to check out my **Free Knitting Patterns** page at **KweenBee.com** . I design new patterns as I get time and add them to my website. I aim to add a couple new ones each month so this list is growing!

To make it even easier, you can take a photo of the QR code below with your phone or tablet. It will take you right to the webpage to see what's new.

If you have printed this pattern... of course, the links won't work! When you are on your favourite search engine like Google, Bing, Yahoo, etc. Enter the term *Kweenbee* and the title as it is written below (capitalization isn't important). It will pop up for you in the search results and be super-easy to find.

For example, enter it like this:

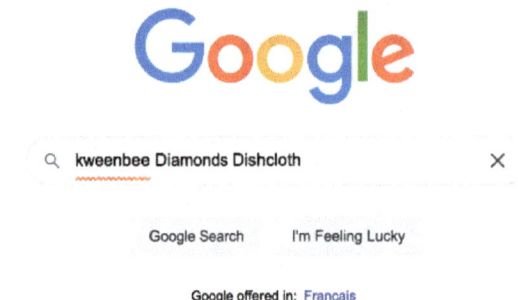

Your results will have my pattern at the very top...usually. Depending on the popularity of the pattern, you may get a link to Pinterest or Ravelry first. Don't worry! All of those options have links back to my original patterns, too!

Fun and Easy Monster Purse

Bulky Yarn Slippers on Straight Needles

How to Knit Spider Fingerless Gloves - Knit Flat on 2 Needles

Winter Beanie Toque or Touque or Tuque with Vertical Stripes

Minimalist Round Toe Slippers – Knit Flat on 2 Needles

One Piece Knitted Dishcloth and Coasters

Knitting for Beginners – Knit a Dishcloth

Easy to Knit Long Cuffed Slippers

Easy to Knit Rolled Cuff Slippers

Knit a Pair of Texting Mitts

Chevron Striped Moccasin Slippers

Super Cozy Textured Adult Bootie Slippers

Textured Easy to Knit Dishcloth Pattern

Super Simple Fingerless Gloves – Knit Flat on 2 Needles

Easy to Knit **OWL** Fingerless Gloves – Knit Flat on 2 Needles

Knit Long Fingerless Gloves – Two Styles with One Pattern

Super Simple Knit Slippers

Follow Me on Social Media

Take a photo with your phone or tablet of the QR codes below. A link will appear. Click the link to go straight to my social media page.

Twitter	YouTube	Threads
Facebook	Instagram	Pinterest
Patreon	My Etsy Shop	Buy Me a Coffee